There is no (
the ONLY wa
learn in a vai
an enjoyable
that will give
Through exciting stories about Kate, Tom
and Sam the dog, **Read with me**:

- *teaches the first 300 key words
  (75% of our everyday language)
  plus 500 additional words*

- *stimulates a child's language and
  imagination through humorous,
  full colour illustration*

- *introduces situations and events
  children can relate to*

- *encourages and develops
  conversation and observational skills*

- *support material includes Practice and
  Play Books, Flash Cards, Book and
  Cassette Packs*

Always praise and encourage
as you go along. Keep
your reading sessions
short and stop
immediately if
your child loses
interest.

A catalogue record for this book is available from the British Library

Published by Ladybird Books Ltd
80 Strand London WC2R 0RL
A Penguin Company

2 4 6 8 10 9 7 5 3 1

© LADYBIRD BOOKS LTD MCMXCIII. This edition MMVI
LADYBIRD and the device of a Ladybird are trademarks of Ladybird Books Ltd

All rights reserved. No part of this publication may be reproduced,
stored in a retrieval system, or transmitted in any form or by any means,
electronic, mechanical, photocopying, recording or otherwise,
without the prior consent of the copyright owner.

ISBN-13: 978-1-84646-360-0
ISBN-10: 1-84646-360-2

Printed in Italy

Ladybird
Read with me
The Space Boat

by **WILLIAM MURRAY**
stories by **JILL CORBY**
illustrated by **TERRY BURTON**

Come here, Kate, please.
Come and look.

Kate and Sam,
come and look.

It's like a boat,
says Kate.

It is a boat,
says Tom.

I have a boat,
says Tom.

Have this, Tom,
says Kate.

Yes, says Tom.

Tom wants a hat.

I want this hat, please, says Tom.

I like this hat,
says Kate.

Come in the boat, Sam,
says Kate.

It's fun.

Yes, here we go,
says Tom.

We want to go up, up,
they say.

They like the boat.

It's fun.
Yes, it's fun in the boat.

Tom, have a look at this, says Kate.

Look at the water.

They go to look at
the water.

Look at the fish, Kate.

Look at the fish
in the water.

We can go to
look at the fish.

No, Sam, no,
not in the water.

You can not go
in the water.

You can't have the fish.

Here they are,
in the boat.

Look at this, Kate.

We can go down.
Down, down they go.

Here are some
for you, Kate.

You have some, Tom.
Here are some for you.

And here are some
for you, Sam.

They go up in the boat.

Sam wants to jump
into a tree.

No, Sam,
you can't jump
into the tree.

Sam wants to jump into the tree.

He can have fun in it.
Sam wants to jump.

No, Sam, you can't jump into it.

Look, says Tom.
I want to go into it,
he says.

Can we go into it,
says Kate.

Here we go, Sam.
Up, up, up.

Here we are.
We can go and look.

Come here, Sam,
says Kate.

We can have fun.

You can't jump,
she says.

Tom looks.

Look at this, Kate, says Tom.

No, no. He can't come into the boat.

Down, Kate, down, Tom says.

Look at Sam,
says Kate.

Sam, no, no.
Down, Sam, down.

You can't jump, Sam.
Come here, please.

I want to go, please, says Tom.

And Sam wants to go.

Yes, says Kate,
I want to go.

Down they go.

Here they are.

It's fun in the boat,
says Kate.

Yes, says Tom.
We like this boat.

Words introduced in this book

Pages	
4/5	come, look, please
6/7	It's, boat, says, It
8/9	have, Have,* this, Yes
10/11	wants, hat
12/13	fun, we, go
14/15	They, they,* to, up
16/17	at, water
18/19	fish, can
20/21	not, You, can't
22/23	are, down, Down*
24/25	some, for
26/27	jump, into
28/29	He
30/31	he*

Number of new words used.....................32

*The same word, with or without a capital letter is shown as it appears in the book.

All are Key Words and are repeated in the following book, Book 4 *Sam to the rescue*.

It's fun in the boat.

What did Tom, Kate and Sam see when they were in the space boat?
Look back in the book to see if you are right.

Ladybird
Read with me
Key Words Reading Scheme

- First Words - A Pre-Reader
- 1 Let's Play
- 2 The Dragon Den
- 3 The Space Boat
- 8 Tom's Storybook
- 9 The Sports Day
- 10 Magic Music
- 11 The Big Secret
- 16 A Busy Night
- Picture Dictionary — Contains 100 Key Words
- 1 Activity Book — Reading, Writing, Listening, Talking